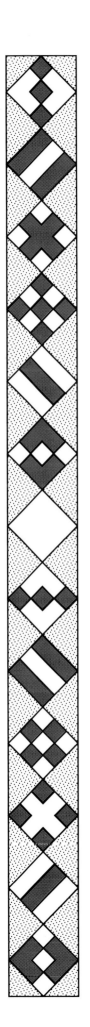

BAKER'S DOZEN DOUBLED

BECAUSE YOU HAVE A LOT OF FABRIC
AND A LOT OF LOVED ONES . . .

by

MARY ELLEN HOPKINS

This book is meant to do a variety of things. First, it provides a brief tutorial of simple pieced block construction for both nine-patches and four-patches. This instruction is supplemental to and supportive of my original "It's Okay If You Sit On My Quilt" book. Second, it provides a lot of (dare I say "hot"?) design ideas I have graphed over a period of a couple of years. Some have been quilted by myself or others. Some of these completed quilts are included in color photographs in this book. The quilters who allowed me to use their work in this book are named and have my undying gratitude (you'll see the great quilts they created.) The designs are reproduced in black and white, which brings me to the final reason for this book. I want you to select your own fabrics and color schemes to make your quilts if you use these designs. Key ideas within particular quilts are indicated where I felt it necessary to do so. Or, maybe these will inspire you to create your own designs. I just know you'll create some masterpieces to share with your family and friends . . . and, just maybe, you'll find you've created your own PPQ (personal private quilt.) Happy quilting!

1

For Lindsey Rose Hopkins
with love from
Grandma Hopkins

CONTENTS

Nine-Patch Construction

Oh, those simple little nine-patches - I call them **Purinas** - make quiet, soothing, and contentment filled hours in your frantic, hectic, wild, and close to insane life.

You'll need:

Whizzy Whacker (otherwise known as a Rotary Cutter!)

Olfa mat

Salem rules (6" x 12" and 4" square)

Stash of fabric visible (out where you can see it)

Ziploc bags

TV in front of sewing machine

Down-Home Rules on fabric choice:

1. DO NOT pull fabric with getting dressed in mind!
2. Value or intensity of colors more important than actual color i.e., light, medium-light, medium, medium-dark, dark.
3. Use several fabrics of same color and value for single round.
4. Mixing different lights together will add a lot of texture.

How to start:

1. Fall in love with 2 or 3 certain fabrics.
2. Choose one of the game plans here.
3. Decide where these 2 or 3 fabrics will go (which round.)
4. Stitch these up.
5. Lay them on the floor and stare at them and then at your visible stash.
6. I only do a round at a time before I make a decision on the next round.
7. Just remember, if you don't have enough of a certain turquoise to complete the round, just look for another turquoise to finish it out. (Use the same color family, as close to the same value as possible. They'll mix very well together.)

Your Personal Private Measurements (PPMs) made by your personal private sewing machine are the keys to a successful quilt top. All machines measure slightly differently from edge of foot to needle. That's all right. Just stick with the same machine during a quilt.

Choosing size of block:

1. A 1" finished grid makes a small 3" block (about 4" diagonal.) The only advantage I can see is that you'll be able to have more rounds.

2. A 1 1/4" finished grid is my favorite size, and will make about a 3 1/2" block (5" diagonal.)

3. A 1 1/2" finished grid is the very largest you should go, I think. This makes a 4 1/2" block (6" diagonal.)

To make a nine-patch, cut strips 1 3/4" wide, the width of the fabric (about 44") using your Salem rule. Sew together as follows, right sides together, edge of your foot always on the edges of your fabric.

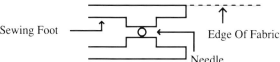

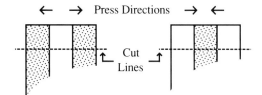

Spend some care on the pressing!

Press seams toward the darker fabric (as shown by arrows) <u>from the right side</u> and as flat as you can make them.

Cut off the selvages on the edges and then proceed to slice into 1 3/4" rows (using 4" square).

Sew these rows together:

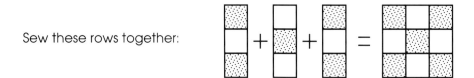

(You will get 24—1 3/4" slices from a set of strips about 44" long.)

Press this little nine-patch and measure from raw edge to raw edge. <u>THIS</u> is your Personal Private Measurement to use for cutting the strips that will be used for your solid squares.

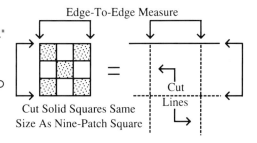

To make

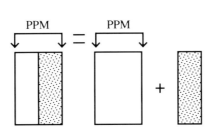

Cut 2 strips light and 2 strips dark, 1 3/4" each. Sew 1 light strip to 1 dark strip. Press seam.

Measure raw edge to raw edge to find your PPM.

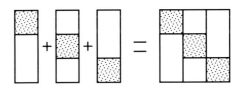

Cut 1 light strip as wide as your PPM and sew to a dark (1 3/4") strip. Press.

Finish Row 2 by adding 1 more light strip next to the dark strip. Press.

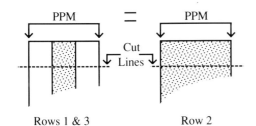

Cut rows into 1 3/4" segments.

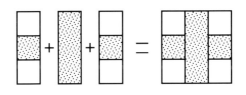

Then sew together to complete the block.

To make

Cut 2 strips light and 1 strip dark, 1 3/4" each. Sew together, dark strip in the middle. Press. Measure raw edge to raw edge to find your PPM, then cut 1 dark strip equal to your PPM.

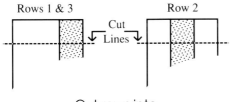

Cut rows into 1 3/4" segments.

Then sew together to complete the block.

To make

Cut 2 strips light and 1 strip dark, 1 3/4" each. Sew together, dark strip in the middle. Press. Measure raw edge to raw edge to find your PPM, then cut into segments your PPM.

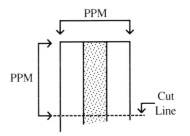

Four-Patch Construction

Behold the four-patch! Now, perhaps you thought those nine-patches were easy. Well, the same principles apply in preparing four-patches as you used in the nine-patches, except there is less to do to make the basic four-patch. The strips are cut the same way, sewn together in the same way, and rows are cut and sewn together in the same way. However, there is one less seam to worry about being lined up when sewing four-patches together.

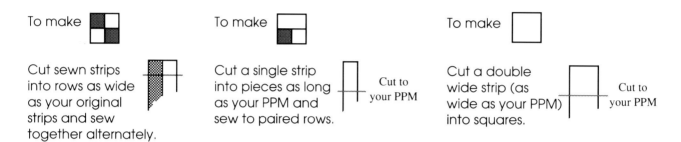

To make ▨ Cut sewn strips into rows as wide as your original strips and sew together alternately.

To make ▨ Cut a single strip into pieces as long as your PPM and sew to paired rows. *Cut to your PPM*

To make ☐ Cut a double wide strip (as wide as your PPM) into squares. *Cut to your PPM*

A trick to use when sewing blocks together is the "twosies and foursies" approach shown below. Note that there is only one seam to line up in the inital block construction instead of two. Also, sewing blocks together in this manner minimizes the length of the edges you have to sew at one time. There will be fewer really long edges, and more shorter edges. It can be frustrating trying to sew several LONG pieces together, especially when they involve a lot of fabric!

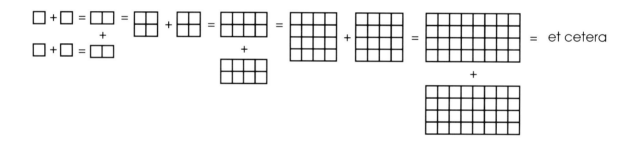

Finishing Touches

Many of these quilt tops are diagonal sets. (Refer to pages 31-33, <u>IT'S OKAY</u> book for further explanation.) The quarter blocks at the end of each row are made as follows:

First, start with one of your fabulous <u>completed</u> blocks.

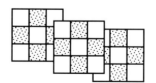

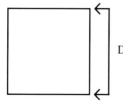

Your block diagonal measure plus 3" equals the side of the large square

Block Diagonal + 3"

Cut squares out of your quarter block fabric with sides equal to your completed block diagonal <u>plus 3 inches</u>.

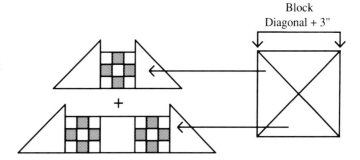

Block
Diagonal + 3"

Now, cut <u>these</u> squares along <u>both</u> their diagonals to get the quarter blocks. Attach these quarter blocks to the ends of your rows before sewing rows together:

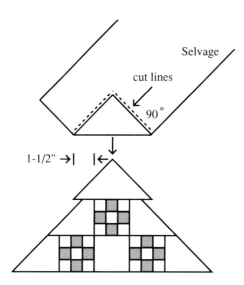

Selvage

cut lines

90°

1-1/2"

After you attach the quarter blocks, and sew the rows together, use a neat technique to get the triangles for the corners of the quilt (see <u>IT'S OKAY</u>, page 30): fold a corner of your selvage over at right angles until the length of the bottom of the triangle extends over the edge of your unfinished quarter blocks by 1-1/2" on both sides; then cut around the sides of the folded triangle to make a square and cut on the folded diagonal to get two corner triangles.

After your quilt top is all together, you can still decide to make it bigger by adding borders. Are your Ziploc sandwich bags getting filled up with all your left over blocks?

Finally, let's see how we can start finishing (that sounds odd, doesn't it?) these quilts. The hardest part is putting the first border on and keeping your quilt "square." I use the technique shown in the figure. First, lay strips of your border on opposite sides of your quilt top (right sides together.) I "eyeball" the straightness. Then measure edge to edge at the top, bottom, and middle so that all three measurements are the same. Then pin the strips down and sew. Isn't that easy? Now do the same to the other two edges of your top. Your quilt is now "square" and will be flat.

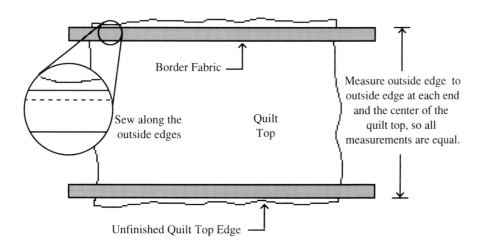

Border Fabric

Sew along the outside edges

Quilt Top

Measure outside edge to outside edge at each end and the center of the quilt top, so all measurements are equal.

Unfinished Quilt Top Edge

Now you can make another top using all those wonderful fabric combinations you came across while hunting for the fabric for <u>this</u> quilt!! It never ends . . .

Let's take a look at some wonderful, hot, and fun designs for quilts you can start on tonight!

LINDSEY ROSE

17
24
8
8
4
10
12
28
32

This is the quilt that I made the evening I heard my first grandchild was on the way. I had to get it cut, layered, quilted, and bound so I could tell the next Hopkins generation that I did this all in one night because I was so excited about becoming a grandmother! Of course, I had to wait nine months to put a name to the quilt! I used some fabrics that were very special to me -- like some off one of the first bolts that I had when I opened my shop. (It may not have been a biggie at the time, but it sure is special now!) This design looks great done up in combinations of plaids, large and small paisleys, combined with other 'overall' prints. My piece is about 40" x 50", but that's because of my own time restriction! Don't you stop here, though. Add your own combinations of purinas, crosses, and 'solid' blocks.

IN THE AIR -- LAX TO NATIONAL MARCH 21, 1987

③

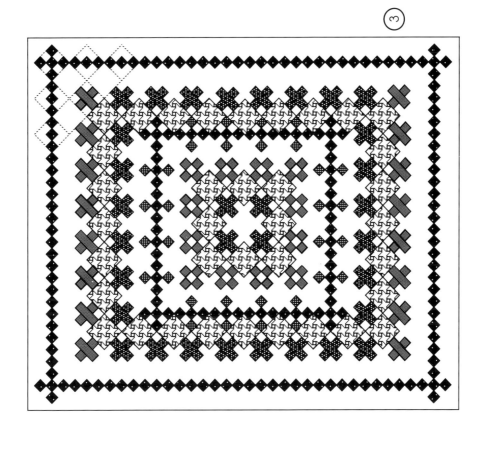

In the spring of 1987, I flew to the East coast for a 13 city speaking engagement. I was on a roll and designed this on the airplane. The speaking tour also got me started on a name for this book!

PATCH AS PATCH CAN # 2

②

This is a variation of Lindsey Rose. The different ways of arranging purinas, crosses, and "solid" blocks could be limitless!

ROOM 1130, SILVER SPRINGS, MARYLAND
MARCH, 1987

30

28

36

32

20

4

24

5

Make sure you use several fabrics of one color for these, otherwise it's too "clunky"!

Can you guess where I was when I did this design?!
Another great design to use lots of plaids, paisleys,
and the wonderful small and large 'one color' prints.
Again I have shown a possible stopping place, and
also given you the option of going on, and on, and.....

DECEMBER 10, 1987 (OFFSET CROSSES)

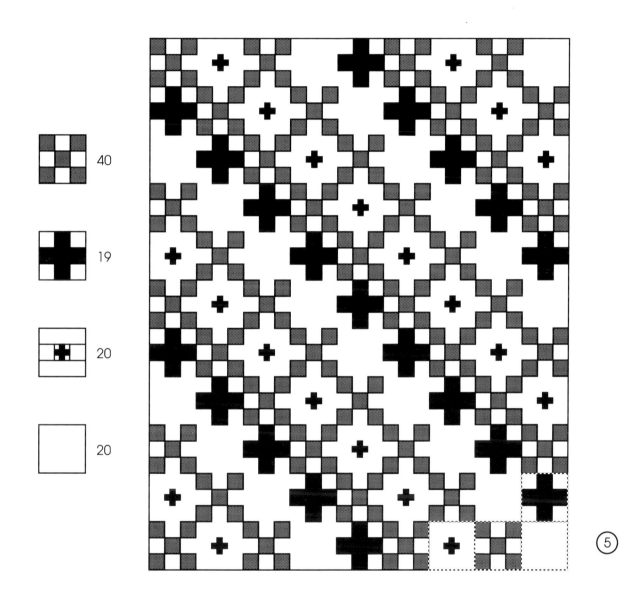

40

19

20

20

(5)

This quilt features the tiny dark crosses framed by nine-patches
and offset from the large dark crosses. It looks neat upright, but tilt
the page and see what happens. And we're talking EASY!

"THE HOMESTEAD"

Hot Springs, Virginia, March 27, 1987

⑥

1 — 28 — 20 — 32 — 28 — 12 — 12 — 80

I suggest using several fabrics of one color for the crosses, and cutting your strips 1-3/4". This will make a finished quilt about 47" x 68", not counting borders or binding.

APRIL 8, 1987

⑦

20 — 12 — 13 — 4 — 12 — 44 — 38 — 36

The key to this quilt is not quite evident here in black and white. Examine the photograph of this quilt and see where the yellow crosses are placed, and color in this design.

12

DECEMBER 9 #2

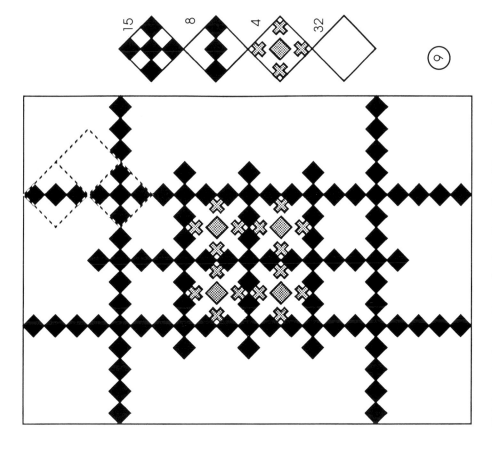

15   8   4   32

⑨

This is a similar pattern, but notice that this one is done ON THE DIAGONAL!

DECEMBER 9 #1

20   4   4   1   34

⑧

This neat little design uses tiny nine-patch crosses as the basis (your initial PPMs) and is straight instead of on the diagonal, so it can be pieced in the twosies and foursies method. But, look at it on the diagonal!

MAY 25, 1987

	13
	16
	68
	10
	32
	28

A design that would look good in patriotic colors, OR anything else you might want to do it up in!!

(10)

MAY 23, 1987

Let's hear it for the Red , White, and Blue--you can really get into the Patriotic spirit with this one! Do it up right in bright reds, whites, and blues.

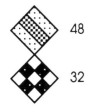

	48
	32

(11)

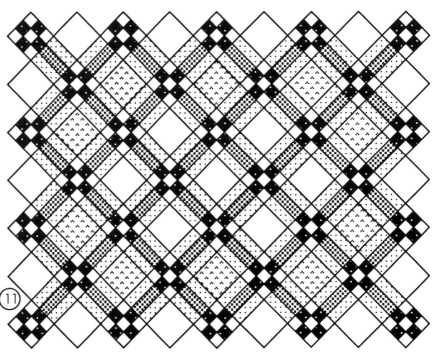

MEMORIAL DAY, MAY 24, 1987

I made my top using Concord printed squares for the nine-patches, stopping at the first "red" round and adding quarter blocks. It measures 38" square. The Concord squares measured 4-1/4" with seam allowance added. Notice the continuing adaptations I've suggested for you. The breakout through the first 'red' round:

Concord printed squares   13

Red with
speckled white   16

White with light red plaid   12

Speckled beiges   20

Different reds   24

HAPPY BIRTHDAY, DAVID HOPKINS!!

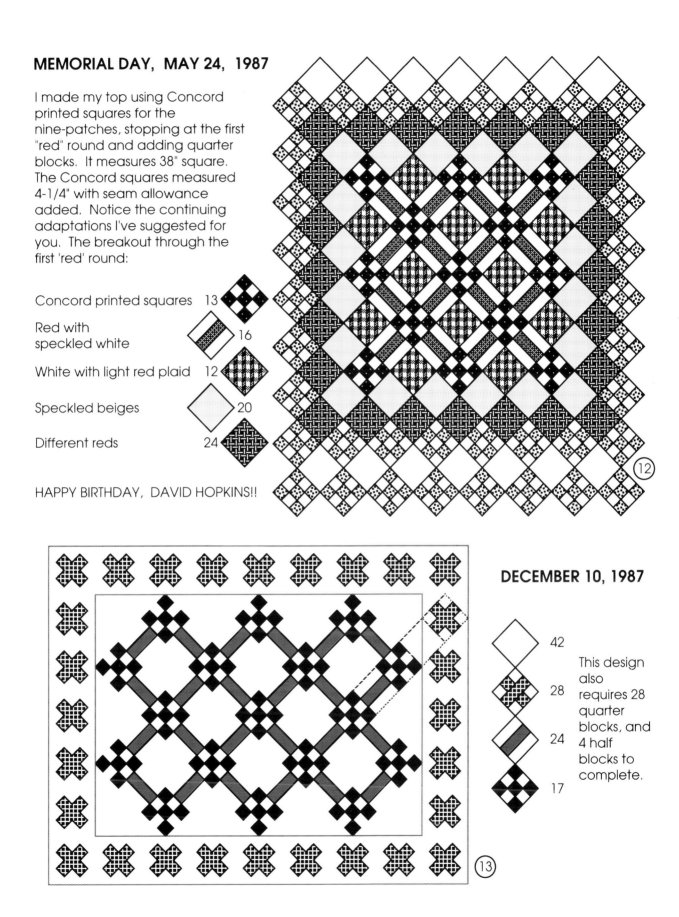

DECEMBER 10, 1987

42

28

24

17

This design also requires 28 quarter blocks, and 4 half blocks to complete.

UTICA, NEW YORK

This quilt was designed in the Sheraton Hotel, Room 431, on April 6, 1987. There are only six purinas in the whole thing! Note the optional treatments on the outside rounds.

(14)

SATURDAY, MAY 23, 1987

The strength of this design is in the ten "X's", formed by dark and medium-dark crosses imbedded in a medium or medium-light background.

(15)

| 53 | 40 | 10 | 20 | 20 |

16

THE ANONYMOUS QUILT

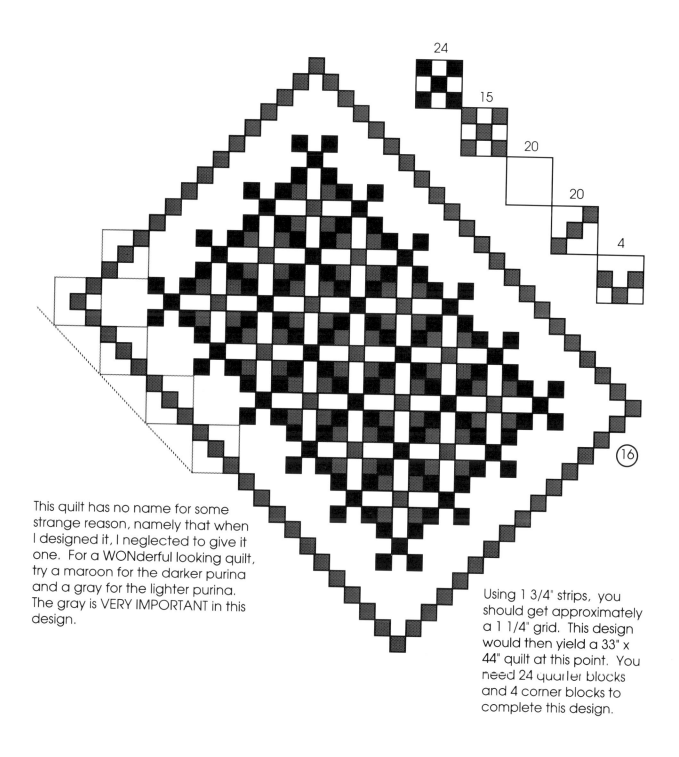

24

15

20

20

4

16

This quilt has no name for some strange reason, namely that when I designed it, I neglected to give it one. For a WONderful looking quilt, try a maroon for the darker purina and a gray for the lighter purina. The gray is VERY IMPORTANT in this design.

Using 1 3/4" strips, you should get approximately a 1 1/4" grid. This design would then yield a 33" x 44" quilt at this point. You need 24 quarter blocks and 4 corner blocks to complete this design.

FRIDAY, MAY 22, 1987

The important feature of this quilt top is the medium-dark diamond surrounding the center design. The look is enhanced by the crown-like corners on the diamond. The quilt can be expanded by including an incorporated border, indicated here in the upper left corner.

	4
	4
	8
	34
	24
	12
	16
	8
	20
	4
	8
	1

LINDSEY ROSE (#1)
PIECED and QUILTED by
MARY ELLEN HOPKINS

MEMORIAL DAY (#12)
PIECED and QUILTED by
MARY ELLEN HOPKINS

LINDSEY ROSE VARIATION
PIECED and QUILTED by
MARY ELLEN HOPKINS

APRIL 8, 1987 (#7)
PIECED and QUILTED by
PAULA FLUDER
PINETREE PATCHWORKS
PUYULLAP, WA

THE HOMESTEAD (#6)
PIECED and QUILTED by
MIMI SHIMP
FOUNTAIN VALLEY, CA

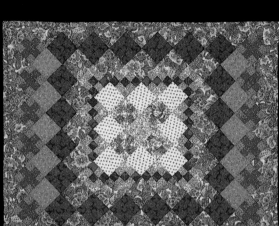

PATCH AS PATCH CAN
VARIATIONS IN MINIATURE
PIECED and QUILTED by
MARTY BARLOND
BARLOND SEWING CENTER
DEARBORN, MI

UTICA, NY (#14)
PIECED and QUILTED by
JAN KRUEGER
HEARTHSIDE QUILTERS NOOK
HALES CORNER, WI

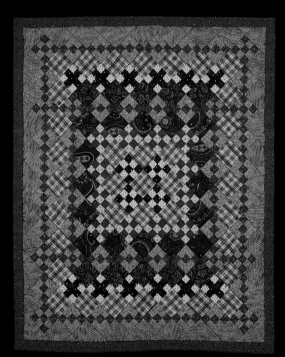

PATCH AS PATCH CAN (#2)
PIECED and QUILTED by
MIMI SHIMP
FOUNTAIN VALLEY, CA

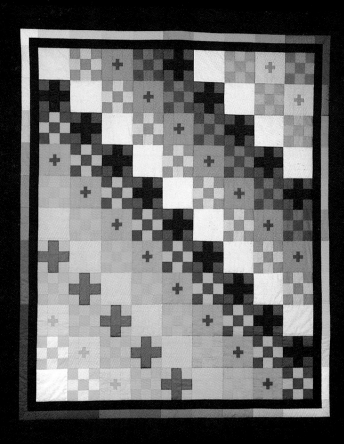

OFFSET CROSSES (#5)
PIECED and QUILTED by
NANCY TAYLOR
GOING TO PIECES
PLEASANTON, CA

FRIDAY, MAY 22, 1987 (#17)
PIECED and QUILTED by
NANCY JACOBY
NANCY J'S
WABASH, IN

APRIL 14, 1987 (#19)
PIECED and QUILTED by
CAMILLE REMME
TORONTO, ONTARIO, CANADA

DOUBLE ARROWHEAD (#20)
PIECED and QUILTED by
JANET HOSSACK
DON MILLS, ONTARIO, CANADA

APRIL 17, 1987 (#18)
PIECED and QUILTED by
KAY PHILLIPS
AGINCOURT, ONTARIO, CANADA

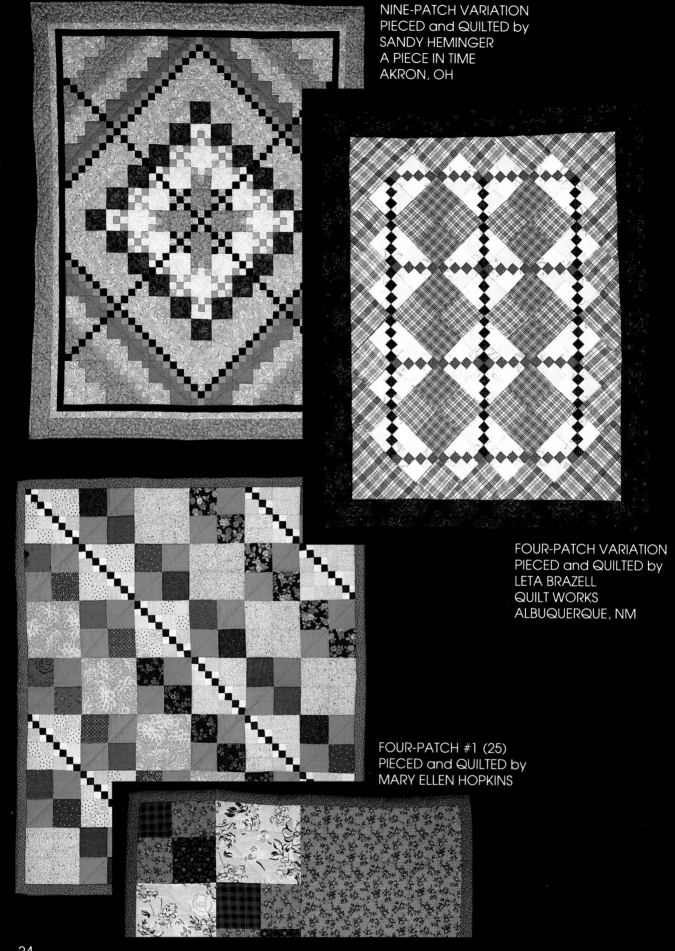

NINE-PATCH VARIATION
PIECED and QUILTED by
SANDY HEMINGER
A PIECE IN TIME
AKRON, OH

FOUR-PATCH VARIATION
PIECED and QUILTED by
LETA BRAZELL
QUILT WORKS
ALBUQUERQUE, NM

FOUR-PATCH #1 (25)
PIECED and QUILTED by
MARY ELLEN HOPKINS

FOUR-PATCH #2 (#26)
PIECED and QUILTED by
MARY ELLEN HOPKINS

FOUR-PATCH VARIATION
PIECED and QUILTED by
CAMILLE REMME
TORONTO, ONTARIO, CANADA

FOUR BY FOUR BY FOUR
-PATCH VARIATION
DESIGNED by JOHN SHIMP
PIECED and QUILTED by
JOHN and MIMI SHIMP
FOUNTAIN VALLEY, CA

THREE CHAIN FOUR-PATCH (#33)
"GOING BANANAS MY WAY"
PIECED and QUILTED by
MIMI SHIMP
FOUNTAIN VALLEY, CA

OFF-SET FOUR-PATCH (#32)
PIECED and QUILTED by
MARY ELLEN HOPKINS

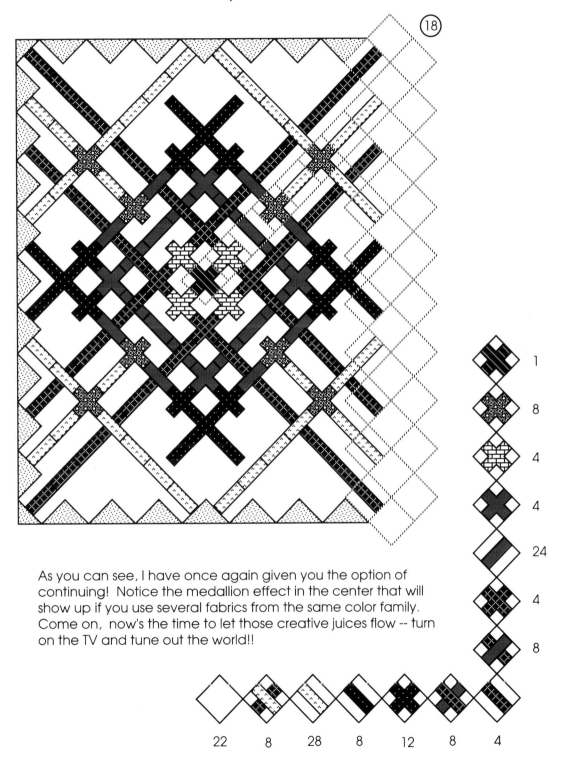

As you can see, I have once again given you the option of continuing! Notice the medallion effect in the center that will show up if you use several fabrics from the same color family. Come on, now's the time to let those creative juices flow -- turn on the TV and tune out the world!!

◇	43
◈	16
◈	8
✖	8
✖	68
◈	52
✖	24

(19)

APRIL 14, 1987

This design requires the number of blocks given if you stop at this point. But you're not going to do that, are you? I didn't think so! Use your imagination and extend the pattern outward.

THE DOUBLE ARROWHEAD QUILT

The things I like best about this quilt are the two different sized arrowheads framing the center. This quilt looks best with different patterns of approximately the same strength for these two rounds.

ANOTHER NINE-PATCH CHAIN

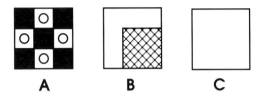

A   B   C

The pattern shown on the right is a
16-block repeat, and . . . what's that you
say? I know, I know! A Baker's Dozen is
13 - well, one thing led to another and I
sort of got carried away. Please try not
to whine. Just to be different let's take
this block and reduce the nine-patch
down to (here's where the "Doubled"
comes in) a four-patch. Look what
happens when you TILT THE PAGE!!

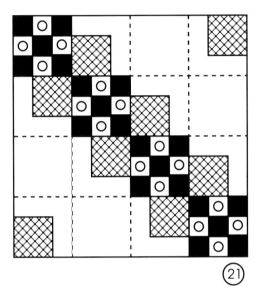

㉑

STUDY NUMBER ONE

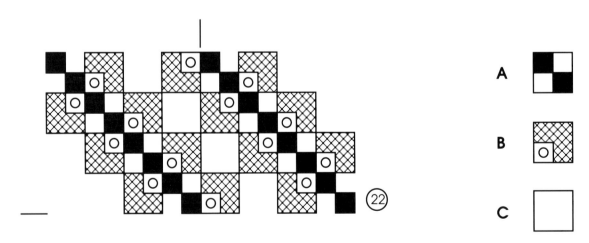

㉒

A

B

C

We still have a 16-block repeat (shown
by the lines above), and the same
fabrics, but it makes an entirely different
quilt.

To make this quilt, let's switch the crissy-crossy and the plain blocks (A and B) and make C a four-patch . . . and then put it all on the diagonal . . .

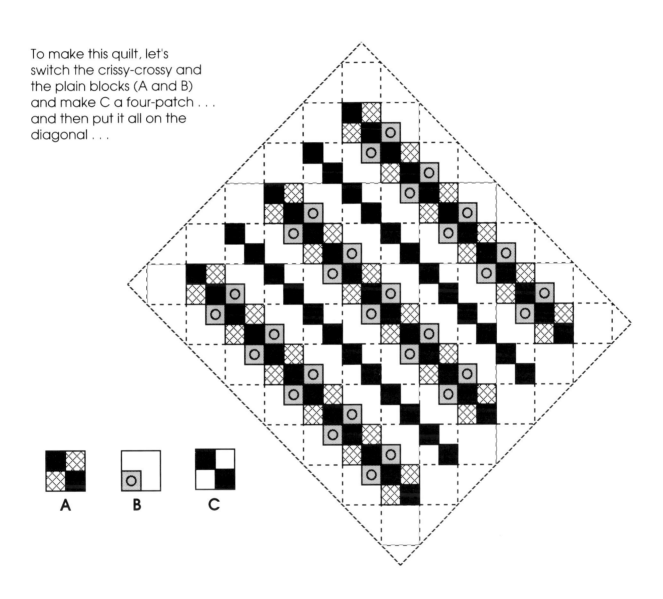

A   **B**   **C**

Not only do these last two quilts look totally different from number 21, but when we went to make it, we found out it was twice as easy (only one seam to line up). So, observing how easy and how much fun four-patches can be, let's turn the page and start playing!

FOUR-PATCH WORKSHEET

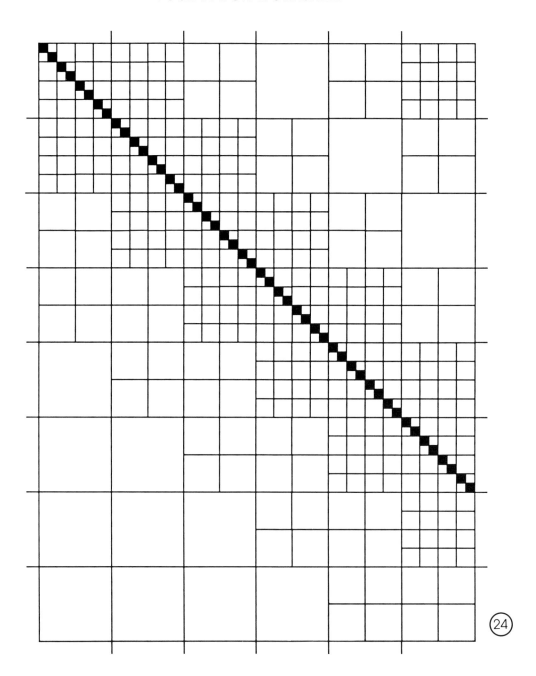

Here is a little worksheet with a pattern using different sized blocks, worked around a single diagonal dark strip. Copy this a few times and try your own color schemes to complete this design. The fun has just begun!

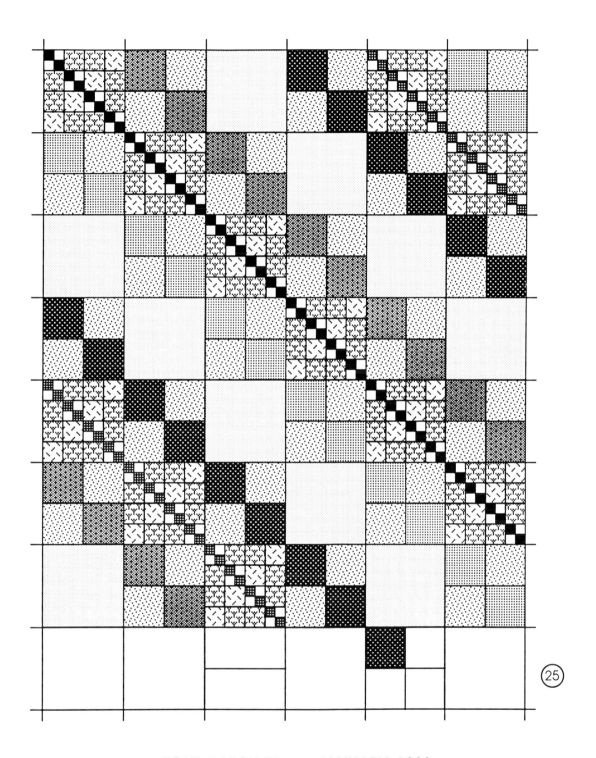

FOUR-PATCH #1 - - - JANUARY, 1988

A very effective treatment for this quilt was to use four colors--black, brown, navy blue, and grape for the smallest four-patches. The remaining rows of four-patches can be done in varying shades of a color--for instance, shades of red or blue diagaonally across the quilt.

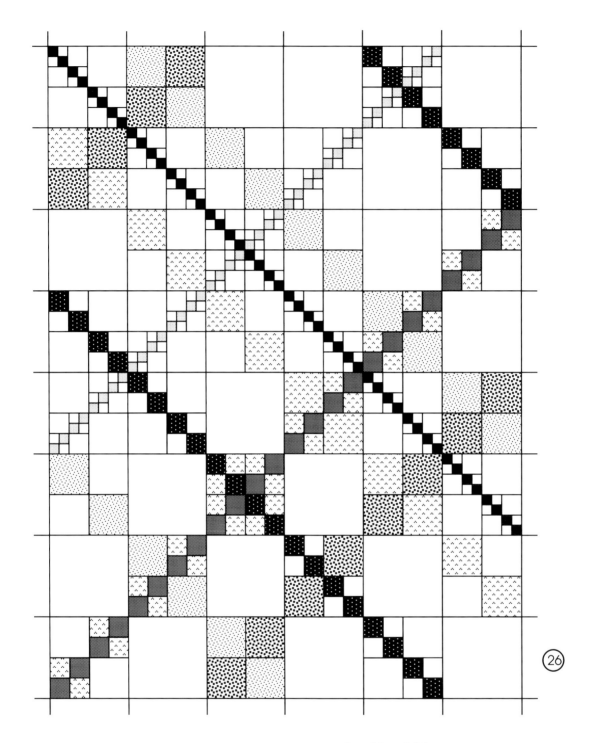

26

FOUR-PATCH # 2 - - - MARCH 23, 1988
QUILTED MARCH 30, 1988

There was a full ziplock bag of the tiny four-patches from #25 and some great lavenders at the shop.......

I really liked the circle that the two medium-size squares made when they criss-crossed. I figure I could make that circle even BIGGER......

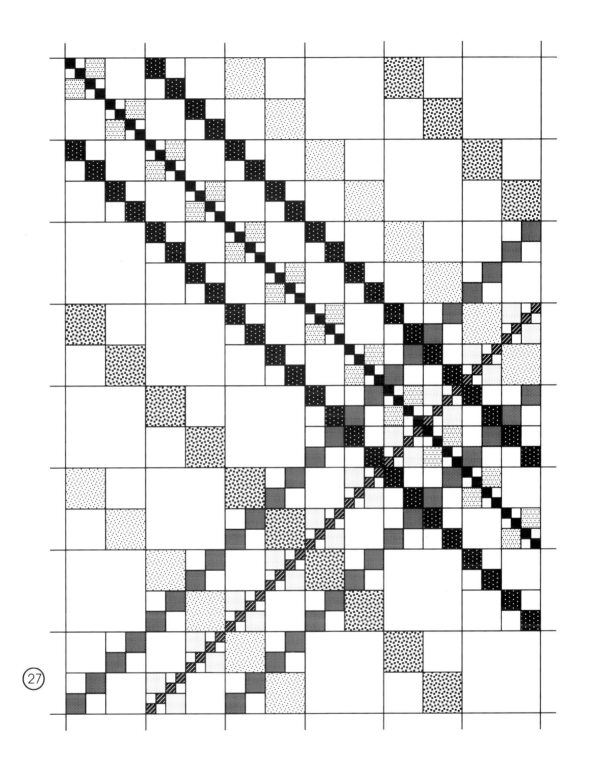

FOUR-PATCH # 3---MARCH 28, 1987

QUILTED MARCH 30, 1987

And sure enough that circle can get bigger!! I liked it so much I made it the back cover!

THE "DRAMATIC LOOK" QUILT TOP

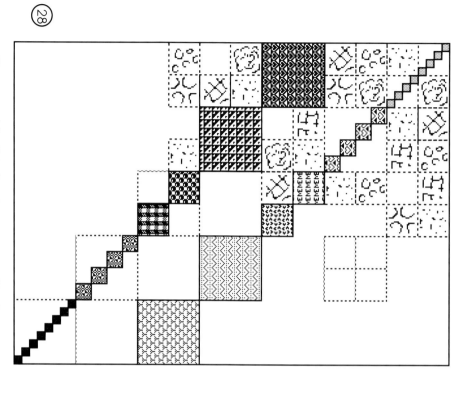

The secret to this simple one: muckled up background squares!! Mix up bones, beiges, tans, grays, creams. If your darts are strong (i. e., one maroon and red, the other one royal and teal) you can use lights AND medium-lights for the background.

FOUR-PATCH # 4

The whole point of this quilt is the center. You too can design dynamite quilts by designing a dramatic center and building outward.

FOUR-PATCH CROSSES

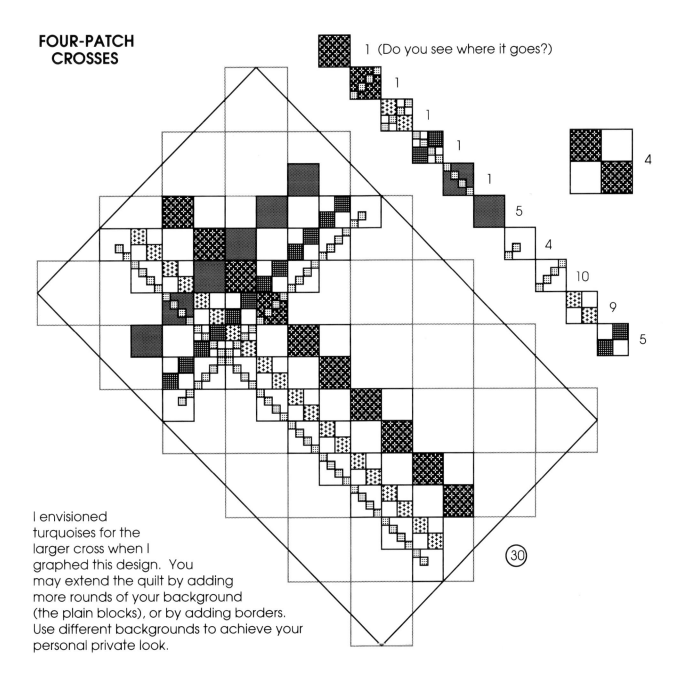

1 (Do you see where it goes?)

1

1

1

1

5

4

10

9

5

4

30

I envisioned turquoises for the larger cross when I graphed this design. You may extend the quilt by adding more rounds of your background (the plain blocks), or by adding borders. Use different backgrounds to achieve your personal private look.

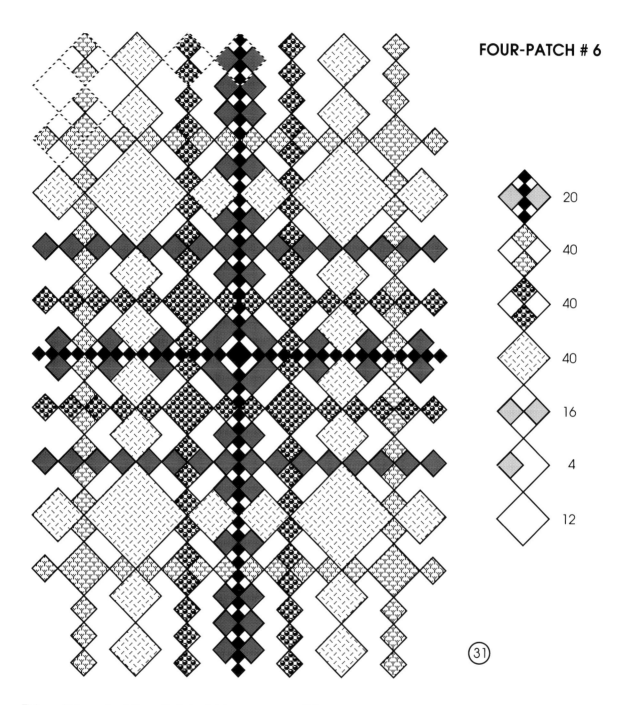

	20
	40
	40
	40
	16
	4
	12

(31)

This quilt is called Four-Patch # 6 because . . . it happens to be the sixth four -patch
I designed! The key to this one is the central cross in a strong color. Note the
horizontal and vertical bar grids (one of each of the second, third, and fourth
blocks shown.) These grids each have the same number of blocks. It might be
fun to see how the overall look changes when the grids are interchanged.

OFF-SET FOUR-PATCH

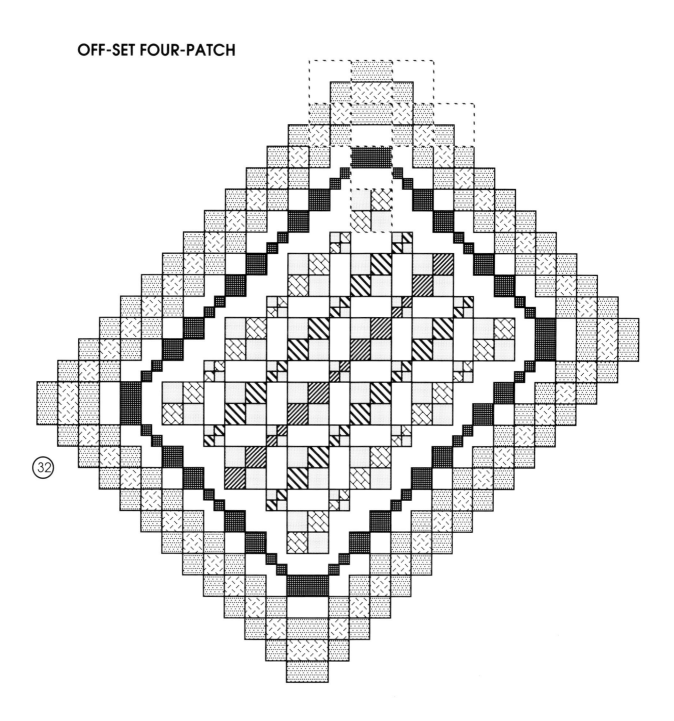

I designed this in January 1988. It was pieced March 29, 1988 and quilted on March 30. The key to this quilt is the muted grays with contrasting colors inset.

THREE CHAIN FOUR-PATCH

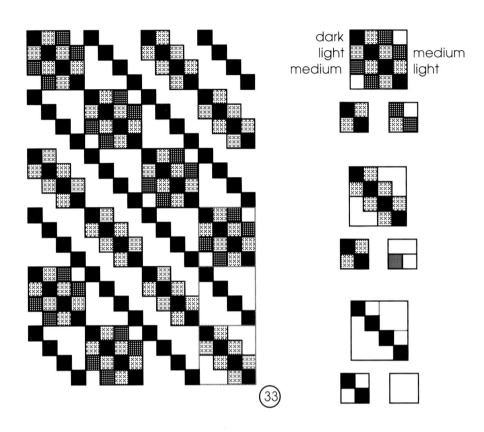

dark
light
medium

medium
light

③③

This quilt uses different shadings of the same colors to get a dramatic look. I graphed this in blues and it looks great. For a 5" block, use 1 3/4" strips (see lower left). This will make approximately a 20" x 30" quilt as shown on the left. For a different look, interchange the light and medium fabrics as shown below.

To make the above quilt:

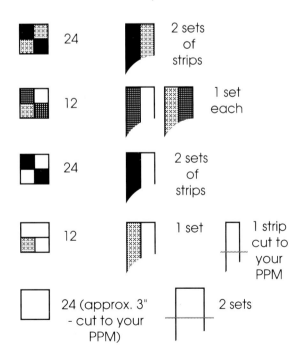

24

12

24

12

24 (approx. 3" - cut to your PPM)

2 sets of strips

1 set each

2 sets of strips

1 set

1 strip cut to your PPM

2 sets

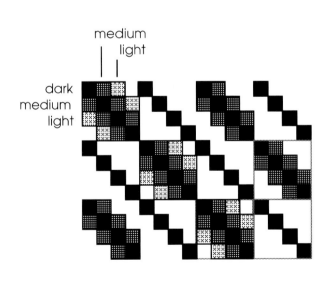

medium
light

dark
medium
light

STERLING CHILDREN'S BOOKS
New York

An Imprint of Sterling Publishing
1166 Avenue of the Americas
New York, NY 10036

ISBN 978-1-4549-1934-6

Distributed in Canada by Sterling Publishing Co., Inc.
c/o Canadian Manda Group, 664 Annette Street
Toronto, Ontario, Canada M6S 2C8
Distributed in the United Kingdom by GMC Distribution Services
Castle Place, 166 High Street, Lewes, East Sussex, England BN7 1XU
Distributed in Australia by NewSouth Books
45 Beach Street, Coogee, NSW 2034, Australia

For information about custom editions, special sales, and premium and corporate purchases,
please contact Sterling Special Sales at 800-805-5489 or specialsales@sterlingpublishing.com.

Manufactured in the U.S.A.

Lot #:
2   4   6   8   10   9   7   5   3   1
08/16

www.sterlingpublishing.com

Design by Heather Kelly

draw
it out

Hundreds of Drawing Prompts to Inspire
CREATIVE EXPRESSION

BRANDON T. SNIDER

INTRODUCTION

Drawing has been a form of expression since Neanderthals were scribbling all over their caves. Now it's YOUR turn to get creative. Read each prompt, take a second to think about it, and then use the space to create whatever your mind interprets it to be. EXPRESS YOURSELF. Feel free to experiment with different styles. Use color, shape, and detail. Draw stuff close up or really far away. HAVE FUN! And if you find yourself stumped, just take a deep breath. When in doubt? DRAW IT OUT!

The perfect pumpkin

A peaceful deer

A bull's-eye with arrows on it

A full head of curly hair | The Easter bunny

A stereo

A frog and a toad who are best friends

A few skyscrapers

Fill this entire page with big circles, small circles, tiny circles, and medium circles

Scrambled eggs with cheese on a plate

_____

An ice cream truck

_____

Oven mitts

_____

A thermos or two

_____

A giant penny

_____

A disgusting breakfast

_____

An interesting
shower curtain

A few delicious-looking
cookies

A pile of tangled
Christmas lights

Fill this page with lots of bubbles.

A pile of walnuts

A four-leaf clover in a field

A surprised armadillo

A chaotic scene

The human brain

A tuba

Three hamsters who are best pals

Some teeth that have never been brushed

A dollhouse with everything in it

Broccoli

A pair of reading glasses

A hot dog with toppings

An old television

A spaceship

A fancy birthday cake

A happy jellyfish | An old anchor | A harmonica

The perfect waterslide

A hilarious bumper sticker

_____

Two boxing gloves

_____

A series of collectible spoons

_____

A pair of red lips

_____

A good birthday gift

Twenty flickering candles

A pair of long johns | A few cinnamon sticks | A bunch of hockey sticks

An exaggerated caricature of a friend's face

An alarm clock

_____

A broken old stapler

_____

A bichon frise

_____

An apple

_____

A catbird

_____

A ten-speed bicycle

_____

A flute | A big thorny bush | A cross-eyed chipmunk

A caterpillar up close

A pan of bacon frying

A pickup truck

A colander

A giant clothespin

A butterfly wing

A man wearing a lot of makeup

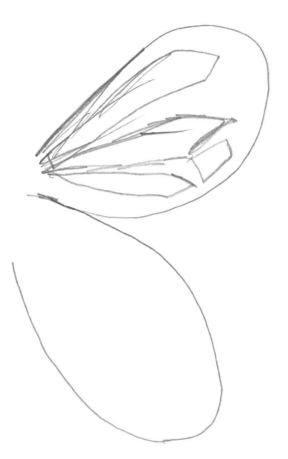

A wishbone or two	A frightened turkey	A gorgeous carnation

A beautiful double rainbow

A pile of pistachio nuts

_____

An old radio

_____

A damsel in distress

_____

A hot dog who can't believe you just said that

_____

An old book

An alien face

A guitar | A rat in a tuxedo | A busy beehive

A very detailed snowflake

A radish that's just been pulled from the ground

Earrings

A decorated cell phone case

A pretzel

A happy lobster

An angry crab

The coolest dolphin you've ever seen

A painter's palette

A pristine marching band uniform

Three shelves of collectible action figures

A peace sign

_____

An ear

_____

A snorkel

_____

A spatula

_____

A weird person

A unique detail on a piece of clothing

A super cool T-shirt

_____

A jar filled with many different candies

_____

A blue rose

_____

A very dirty dog

A hammock

_____

A fresh banana and a not-so-fresh banana

_____

Three unique pencils

_____

A basketball

_____

A clown

A fairy princess

Something you might find in a swamp

_____

A pirate head

_____

An exotic coral reef

_____

A movie poster of your favorite movie

A plate of piping hot biscuits and gravy

_____

A funny air freshener

_____

A kitchen sink filled with dirty dishes

_____

Lots of feathers

_____

A handful of nickels

A shark jumping out of the ocean

An antique lamp	A table full of votive candles	A Pomeranian

Write your name in a hundred different ways.

A pile of almonds

A horseshoe

An ancient king laughing

A large boulder

A logo that represents your family

The palm of your hand

A blue jay sitting on
a tree branch

A bubbly soda

Three gerbil friends

A multi-panel comic strip about something that happened to you

Lettuce

_____

A fancy necklace

_____

A piano

_____

An iron

_____

The best gift you've ever received

An evil sorcerer

A scary teddy bear | A melting ice cream cone | A rolled-up yoga mat

A famous monument that you think is pretty cool

A tiny cottage on a mountainside

_____

A skillet

_____

Two bright eyes

_____

A killer whale

_____

A sad man

An oddly shaped watermelon

An ugly hat | A holiday wreath | A bunch of limes

An underwater vista filled with fish

A brand new tennis racket

_____

A rug with an intricate design

_____

A Boston terrier

_____

A used eraser

_____

A hippo mixed with a giraffe

_____

A house covered in Christmas lights

_____

Something you might find in
a doctor's office

Seagulls attacking
a bagel

A bunch of seaweed

Fill this page with big squares, small squares, tiny squares, and medium squares.

A pile of sausage links

_____

A cool sports car

_____

A fancy candelabra

_____

A small BBQ grill

_____

A sunflower in full bloom

Two dolls in funny poses

A first aid kit | Different kinds of gift wrap | A sweet peony

A three dimensional box

A cute little ladybug

A helicopter

Bigfoot drooling

A pile of sunflower seeds

A peaceful scene

A mini pony

A bat with its wings spread

Two perfect carrots

A cardinal wearing a chef's hat

A very hairy leg

A harp

A pair of dirty socks

A plate of hot nachos and cheese

A unique bottle opener

Someone laughing hysterically | Scary lightning

A bucket of clams | A skeleton | A paper airplane

A very surprising scene

A smiley face

An epic-looking sword

A surfboard with a cool original logo

A single finger in detail

An excited snail   A clarinet

A roll of toilet paper | A Pilgrim hat | An orchid

An exaggerated caricature of yourself

A picture frame containing
a photo you're fond of

A bunch of grapes

A notebook covered in doodles

A classic football

Fill this space with paisley designs.

Santa Claus

Something you might find in a locker

A greasy fried chicken leg

Algae

An insect up close

A bowl of cereal

An old pocket watch

A box of tissues

A pair of garden shears

An open treasure chest

A jar of change

A drying rack

_____

A polka-dot bow

_____

A cute pug

_____

A sky full of clouds

A basket full of water balloons

Four hazelnuts

A scooter in motion

A tiny haunted house

A nasty witch
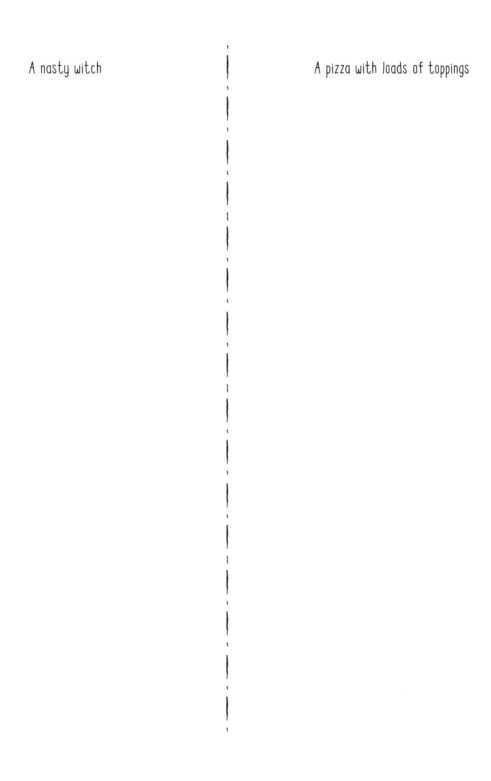
A pizza with loads of toppings

A frantic turkey | An antique violin | A bunch of meerkats popping their heads above ground

A spooky jack o' lantern

A beet sliced in half

_____

A long scarf

_____

A candy bar with its wrapper half off

_____

A flashlight

_____

A cruise ship

Some dyed Easter eggs

A puffer fish

_____

A Viking helmet

_____

An old-looking photo of two best friends

_____

A statue of your favorite mythical creature

A stop sign

A button

A single toe in detail

A deflated volleyball

A mean cat

A variety of soup ladles

Deodorant

_____

A fresh apple pie

_____

A few Chihuahuas

_____

A complicated maze

A mango

A toothbrush that's been used a lot

A few golf clubs

A pile of paper clips

A snowman   A bear mixed with a snake

Something you might find at a water park

A baby fox

Warm mashed potatoes covered with butter

Your favorite painting

A piece of toast with jam and butter | A bunch of steel wool

A minivan covered in graffiti | The face of a wristwatch

An oddly shaped chair and a regular chair

A bunny rabbit in motion

A rainbow spoon

_____

Lots of sparkling tinsel

_____

Lavender

_____

A chain-link pattern that fills the page

A punk

Some fancy luggage

A pair of dice

A cashew nut

A suspension bridge in profile

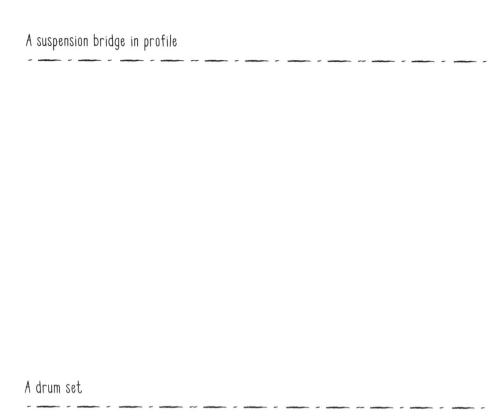

A drum set

A chatty toucan | Frankenstein | An opossum that's been caught climbing out of a garbage can

A fully decorated Christmas tree

A pair of sunglasses

A plate of chicken fingers

A bib with a clever catchphrase on it

A cauliflower

Someone crying | A headless horseman

Two sea horses having a chat

A crossbow

A terrible wedding cake

A regal sand castle

A line of musical notes

_____

A strainer

_____

A baby's foot

_____

A shuttlecock

_____

A hero

A sturdy backpack

A long whistle

A mailbox

A lotus

A jungle scene

A kid's comb

Two different size tomatoes

Scissors

Swimming goggles

A crystal ball that shows the future

A stressed-out gingerbread man

Something you might
find at a mall

A pile of mushrooms

A pie chart

Fill this page with big triangles, small triangles, tiny triangles, and medium triangles.

Hash browns

_____

A luxurious couch

_____

A pair of tongs

_____

A one-dollar bill

_____

Curtains | Funky triplets

Binoculars

A bunch of bells

A hungry poodle

A map of Africa

A pile of pecans

An old stamp

A sleepy ninja

A cat box with poo in it

A welcoming home | A funky hairstyle

A saxophone

A rooster dressed
like a superhero

A raccoon wearing
reading glasses

A very wrinkly face

Spinach

Two different gloves

A bowl of gummy bears

Medicine

A scene that you hope
happens in the future

A device you just invented off the top
of your head that will save the world

A happy sea lion

_____

A scene from your favorite cartoon

_____

An attractive garden

_____

A scene that makes you furious

A heart

A couple of strange forks

A belly button up close

A fishing lure

A villain   An overflowing trash can

A beautiful old lantern | A special ornament | An inflatable baseball bat

A table set for Thanksgiving dinner

A microwave   A moldy peach

A stack of important papers   A drooly dachshund

A butterfly mixed with a pig   A fearless explorer

A brand-new toy chest

_____

An eggplant

_____

A lamb

_____

A tarantula up close

A bowl of delicious fruit

A broom

A sweet racecar

A worn sneaker

A raincoat

A tiny woman wearing a large hat

A bunch of grocery
bags filled with stuff

A person in a
hot dog costume

A daffodil

A spinning globe

A chainsaw

Medusa

Dracula

A pile of Brazil nuts

A dozen lightning bugs

_____

A cheetah

_____

A weeping willow tree

An antique banjo

A parrot

A top hat

Soap

A brush that's full of hair

Celery

Fill this page with pieces of popcorn.

The worst gift you've ever received

An original superhero that
you just came up with a second ago

An ax

A muscular gladiator

Something you
wish you owned

Your dream backyard

A sign that reads "DO NOT ENTER"

An ice cube tray

Bushy eyebrows

A goldfish

A water lily

A zipper pull

Sunscreen | A pinecone | A majestic tree during the summer

A happy family

A blueberry

A barbell

A pair of nail clippers

A paint brush

Fill this space with magical sparkles.

A dragon with one tooth

A pile of toy blocks | An expensive vase | A squirrel taking a nap

A brand-new thing you just created in your head

Oatmeal with maple syrup on top

_____

Tweezers

_____

A shelf with stuff on it

_____

The grossest foot you can imagine

_____

The most awesome kite ever   A curly straw

A recycling symbol

A candy cane

A Yorkshire terrier

A wheelchair in profile

A five-dollar bill

A bunch of French fries in bed

A peach pit with arms, legs, and a face, escaping from a peach

---

Your best friend in profile

A mummy

A sturdy pine tree | An aloe vera plant | A shiny French horn

A wall of shelves with books and a couple of surprises

A spilled can of soda

_____

An ear of corn

_____

An interesting cane

_____

A juicy cheeseburger

_____

Your favorite toy

Your favorite meal

A bunch of stacked tin cans | An old queen | A tube of toothpaste

Three unique cacti

An error message

A nose

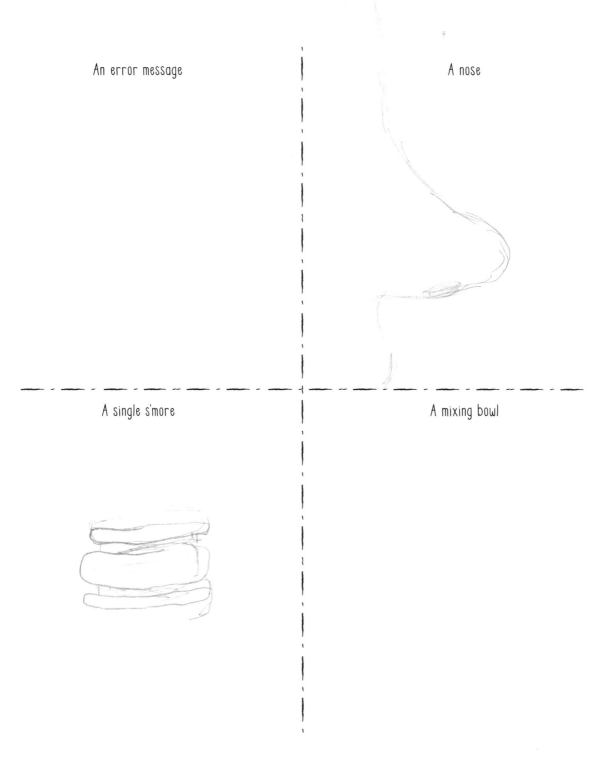

A single s'more

A mixing bowl

A confused person   A city skyline

Lip balm

———————————————————————————————————————

A badly wrapped gift

———————————————————————————————————————

A greyhound

———————————————————————————————————————

A roller coaster with a lot of twists and turns

A coconut that's just been split open

A flounder

A notebook covered in scribbles

Some tennis balls in a fun formation

A shark mixed with a mouse   Amelia Earhart

A dart board

_____

Three snails racing

_____

A bunch of creeping vines

_____

Fill this page with big pentagons, small pentagons, tiny pentagons, and medium pentagons.

A full plate of pancakes

_____

An air conditioner

_____

A monster truck

_____

A sky full of fireworks

_____

A pair of beat-up boots

A very pimply face

A tiger lily in a flowerpot | A pack of bungee cords | A beautiful holiday poinsettia

The lower half of a face with a big toothy smile

A goblin queen

Chestnuts roasting on an open fire

An angry bull's head

Something gross

An unsafe place | The Wolfman

A bikini top and bottom

_____

A couple of gourds

_____

A bunch of daisies

_____

Six rows of people watching a baseball game

Lots of peas

A spicy sausage

A baby rattle

A barrette

A kayak with two kayakers

A full Easter basket

A cyborg warrior | A string of Chinese paper lanterns | Two squids shooting ink at one another

The best scene ever

An antique key

A cookbook

A single tooth

A piece of sushi

A frightened dinosaur

A necktie with a colorful print

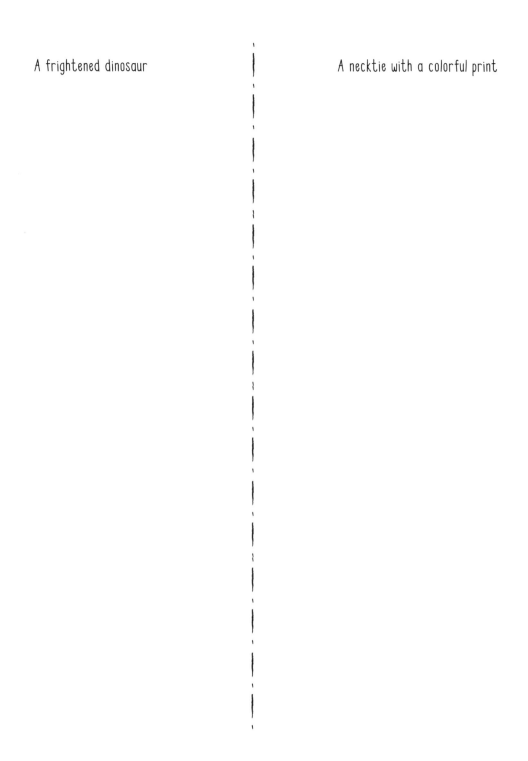

A bunch of batteries | A stocking filled with stuff | A wilted petunia

Fill this page with lots of different cupcakes.

An assortment of presents

_____

A golden check

_____

A magic scroll with an ancient spell written on it

_____

A subway map

A flaming skull

A triangle instrument | A wasp's nest | A tower of crayons

A bumblebee up close

A complete bedroom set

A cooler filled with stuff

A bowl of delicious grits

A stove in use

A futuristic hairstyle

A twenty-dollar bill

An antique canteen

A funny cookie jar

A peanut butter cup

A sandal

A complicated pattern that repeats in rows across the page

Peanuts

A sleek airplane

A cyclops

Wind chimes

A rhinoceros head | A galactic empress

A fern | A hot air balloon | A shocked duck

The perfect outfit

A raw onion

A child's favorite blankie

A storm of candy

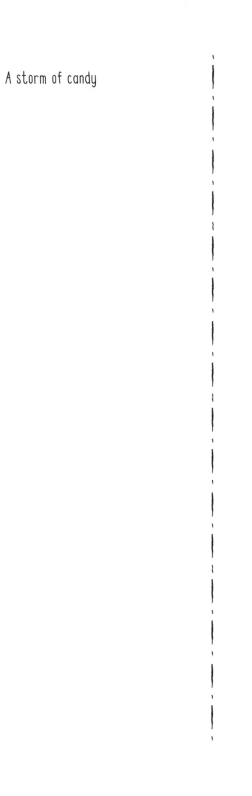

A room in a castle

Something you think is seriously uncool

_____

A manta ray

_____

A court jester

_____

Something you fear greatly

A danger sign

A complicated tent

A turkey baster and
a frightened turkey

Lots of paw prints

A belt buckle

A bad attitude

A showerhead | A little devil | A Maltese

An ant farm

A few kiwis

A strangely shaped lightbulb

An autographed soccer ball

An exciting tape dispenser

A lizard mixed with a peacock

A website

A tambourine

A lovable panda

A skinny chameleon

A totally original poster for a movie you just created in your head

Four eggs sunny-side up

_____

A fire alarm

_____

A tricked-out limousine

_____

A few sturdy padlocks

_____

A peacock with its feathers in full display

A pile of nails

A thermometer | A very ugly sweater

A map of a fictional place

A robot

A booger

A computer keyboard

Something you hope
no one will see

A grid of tiny pentagons

A pirate ship

A cello | A very large jade plant | An injury

A full head of hair showing every single strand

A nice bracelet

A slice of pizza

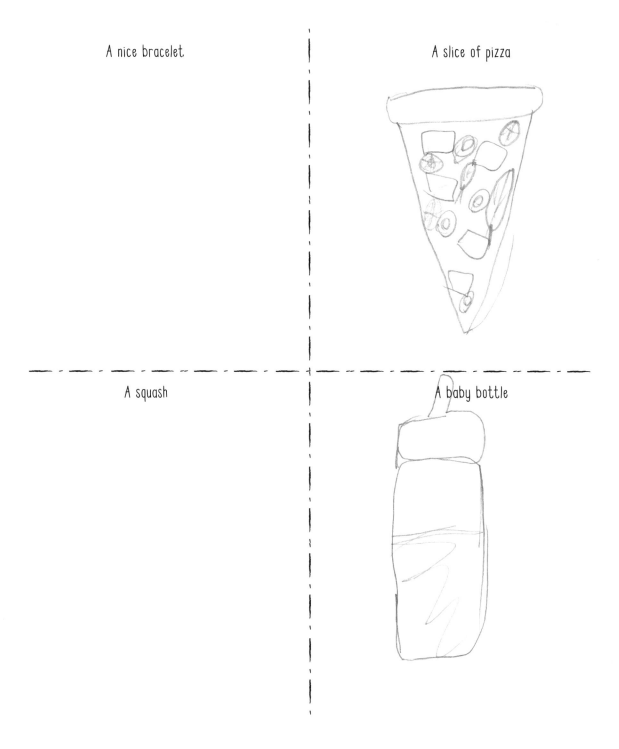

A squash

A baby bottle

A mythical beast

The most embarrassing thing

A cable car

_____

A swarm of angry bees

_____

An electric eel who wants to kiss you

_____

A wall of Egyptian hieroglyphics

A box of cereal

An armpit

Burnt toast

A protective shield

Something that has brought you great joy in your life

Something that annoys you to no end

A decorative bath mat

_____

A fawn

_____

A luscious hibiscus

_____

Fill this page with stars of a million different sizes.

A television playing a scene
from a show you love

Give yourself an entirely
different look, complete with new
hair, clothes, and attitude.

A brand-new trumpet
_____

A famous flag
_____

A smiling hedgehog
_____

A self-portrait on your best day